# basic
# CHORDS
# FOR GUITAR

Other titles available by David Mead from Sanctuary Publishing:

*Basic Scales For Guitar*
*Basic Guitar Workout*
*100 Tips For Acoustic Guitar*
*100 Guitar Tips You Should Have Been Told*
*Rhythm – A Step By Step Guide To Understanding Rhythm For Guitar*
*10 Minute Guitar Workout*

With Martin Taylor
*Kiss And Tell – Autobiography Of A Travelling Musician*

For all of the latest information about David Mead's books, clinics and concert appearances, check out www.davidmead.net.

Printed in the United Kingdom by MPG Books, Bodmin

Published by Sanctuary Publishing Limited, Sanctuary House, 45-53 Sinclair Road, London W14 0NS, United Kingdom

www.sanctuarypublishing.com

ISBN: 1-86074-363-3

# basic
# CHORDS
# FOR GUITAR

**DAVID MEAD**

# contents

## section 1
## chapter 1

## chapter 2

## chapter 3

........................................................

## **section 2**
## chapter 4

........................................................

# chapter 5

# introduction

Learning to play some chords is the first really big hurdle faced by students new to the guitar. The purpose of this book is to look at the task of becoming familiar with the process from the ground up. I'm going to present you with a plan for learning everything with one basic thought in mind: we're going to do everything in the right order. A lot of chord tutors make the mistake of coming across more like a dictionary – all chords are given equal space, with no direction as to how to go about learning things with any kind of strategy in mind.

You may find that you've already covered a lot of ground already, in which case you'll be able to benefit from how the book has been sectionalised into chord families: major, minor and sevenths. This will enable you to use the book as a reference guide as you progress with your guitar playing.

If you're a beginner, I'd advise you to pay special attention to the first few chapters. These are laid out progressively and take into account the fact that your hand has to go through a few biological changes before certain things are possible for you. For instance, certain muscles have to be allowed to develop, and this takes time, just as it would if you were doing exercises in a gym. Certain things will become easier as you go along, and it's certainly not advisable to do too much too soon – this is the path towards frustration, and that's one thing we want to avoid. After all, playing the guitar is meant to be fun!

*David Mead*
*Spring 2002*

# section one

# how to read chord boxes

In order for you to make the most of the information contained in this book, I'm going to spend a few minutes to explain what's what in the diagrams I've used for the chords. Just think of it as essential orienteering.

First, you need to know the names of a few of the guitar's bits and pieces, just to be sure that we're all talking the same language. Take a look at the diagram below:

This piece of plastic (it used to be bone in the early days) is called the *nut* and marks the end of the guitar strings' journey down the fretboard. On the other side of the nut (ie to your left) you'll find the tuning pegs, sometimes known as the *machine heads*. Meanwhile, the playing surface of the guitar is known as the *fretboard* or *fingerboard*.

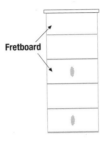

**Fretboard**

The next thing to learn the names of are the *frets*, or the pieces of metal that lie across the fretboard:

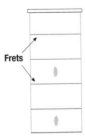

**Frets**

Now all we have to do is shrink things down a little and add six strings and we've got ourselves a fully fledged and recognisable chord box, just like the ones found in the rest of this book:

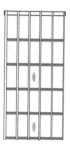

The strings go from the thickest, on the left-hand side of the diagram, to the thinnest, on the right. This diagram shows what you see when you're looking at your guitar face-on, as if it were standing up in front of you. The notes to which the strings are tuned are as follows:

E   A   D   G   B   E

And so the complete picture would look something like this:

In order to show you where exactly to put your fingers on the fretboard to play a chord, we use black circles, like this.

In order to indicate which left hand finger is to be used to fret the note, there is a number underneath the relevant string, like this:

**C major**

3  2     1

The fingers are numbered out from the thumb so that your index finger is 1, middle finger is 2, ring finger is 3 and little finger (or pinkie in the USA) is 4. This numbering convention holds for just about everything the left hand does on the fretboard, so it's definitely worth committing it to memory from the outset. (The name of this particular chord is shown above, but don't worry about that at the moment; this diagram is just to ensure that you've got the basic idea.)

In order to sound the clearest note possible, you need to position your fingers very close to the fret, as shown here:

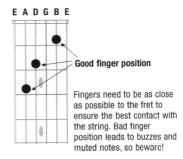

**E A D G B E**

**Good finger position**

Fingers need to be as close
as possible to the fret to
ensure the best contact with
the string. Bad finger
position leads to buzzes and
muted notes, so beware!

When you play a chord, you're not always expected to
play every string. Sometimes you have to leave strings
out of the chord because they won't sound right if you
play them. When this happens, you'll see a little "x"
over the top of the string that isn't played.

When this appears, it's usually one of the bass strings
that you're meant to leave alone, and so for this chord
you'd be expected to play only the five strings to the
right of the diagram:

**Don't sound this string**

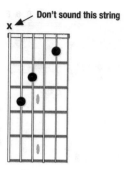

On the other hand, sometimes you are meant to play strings that don't have fingers on them. We call these *open strings*, and they are indicated by a little "o" above the string.

In this chord, there are three strings that are meant to remain open.

**how to read chord boxes**

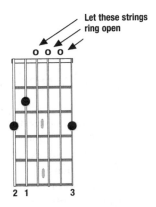

Let these strings ring open

# buzzy logic

If you've tried to play a few notes and found that all you get is a buzzy, unclear note or one that's muffled and not really a note at all, you'll have to do a little bit of experimentation with finger position and pressure. You don't need to grip the guitar neck like you would if you were hanging from a trapeze, though; this will actually prevent your hand from moving freely over the fretboard and forming chord shapes.

You don't have to press too firmly with your fingers, either. The only way you'll find out exactly how much pressure to apply is by practising a few chord shapes,

19

making adjustments as you go, until everything is crystal clear.

# wounded in action

While we're on the subject of digits, one of the facts of guitar-playing life is sore fingertips. This particular soft flesh never thought it was going to have to hold guitar strings down and the result is peeling skin and blisters. But – and I'm aware that I'm not painting too pretty a picture here – you'll soon find that the skin hardens up and ceases to be a problem. The important thing to remember is that the only way to ensure that hard skin replaces the soft is to keep on playing!

# position markers

You've probably noticed the dots or spots on the fretboard of your guitar and wondered if they have any musical significance, like the black notes on the piano keyboard. They don't. They're really just there as a visual guide, some landmarks to let you know where you are. If they weren't there, the guitar fretboard would look a very lonely place indeed. The dots or spots are known as *position markers* and fall at the third, fifth, seventh, ninth and twelfth frets, something like this:

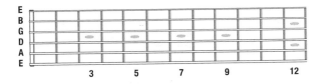

From there on, they continue on the 15th, 17th, 19th and, if your fretboard is long enough, the 21st.

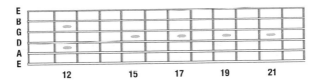

Throughout this book, I've included little figures by some of the chord boxes to let you know which fret you're meant to line your fingers up with – and they look like this:

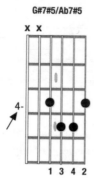

The diagram above tells you that you're meant to line the blobs up with the fourth fret. Remember that there's a position marker on the fifth fret, so you've only got to move next door. This saves you counting up from the bottom of the guitar neck every time you need to locate your fingers.

# which way is up?

Two things that prove most confusing to players new to the guitar concern a bit of basic geography. If we talk about the guitar's "bottom string", we are in fact talking about the one nearest you when you're holding the guitar in a playing position.

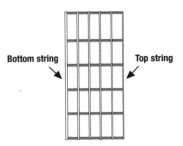

**Bottom string** → 　　　← **Top string**

This is because it's the string that carries the bottom – or lowest – notes found on the instrument.

Similarly, when we talk about going "up" the fretboard, we mean going from left to right as you hold it in a playing position – ie, towards the body.

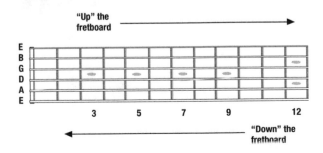

"Up" the fretboard →

3　5　7　9　12

← "Down" the fretboard

23

The reason for this is that, if we go in this direction, the notes get higher. In other words, they're going up in pitch.

If all of these names and various bits and pieces sound really confusing to begin with, don't worry – you'll soon get used to them!

# the right way to learn

The purpose of this chapter is to make sure that you take your all-important first steps in playing chords in the right order. The most important thing to remember when you're learning something new is not to take too much on at once. This is exactly why we're going to spend a little time on the nursery slopes, making sure everything is developing nicely, before trying any more risky manoeuvres. By the end of this chapter, you should be prepared to tackle all of the chords in the second section of this book and the door to your progress as a chord wrangler will be wide open.

If you've read the chapter on how to read chord boxes, you'll have a good idea of what goes where already, but you shouldn't try to rush ahead too soon. There's nothing more frustrating than trying to play your first chord and finding that your fingers just won't sit on the fretboard properly or that some of them won't reach where they're meant to be. Your hand will have to develop a few of its muscles, and it will have to stretch a little, too, so don't be surprised if a few of those chords listed in the back of this book seem impossible to play at first.

The other factor worth considering here is that I'm taking for granted that you're right handed. (If you're left-handed, please read the section "Left In The Wilderness?" below.) Therefore, your "fretboard" hand isn't used to doing too much at all and will take time to come out of hibernation. This is why it's important to tackle things in the right order, so that this natural development can progress at a steady pace.

# left in the wilderness?

"Oh dear! You're left handed, aren't you?" Is this the reaction you received when you bought your first guitar? Maybe you even got the lecture about there being no such thing as a left-handed piano or a left-handed typewriter, too, thrown in for good measure. The fact is that being a left-handed guitarist in a right-handed world can be a serious disadvantage – you nearly always end up paying more for your instruments and guys like me don't write left-handed guitar tutors like we should, so almost everything can become seriously topsy-turvy – as if you've not got enough problems already!

In my experience as a teacher, I've come across only a very few left-handed players who actually decide to play the guitar the other way around. (Notice that I didn't say the wrong way around.) Generally, if I can get to them early enough, I tell them that being left-handed and playing guitar in the conventional way is actually an advantage.

Think about it. You do all those awkward, detailed little jobs like holding a pen, a screwdriver, a tennis racket, snooker cue or whatever with your left hand because that's what your brain is telling you is the correct orientation for you, so when it comes down to playing guitar the temptation is to play the opposite way around from a right hander, just the same way as you would with practically everything else, because you think that you should. But stop for a second, because it might not make the difference that you think it might.

When you think about it, right-handed guitarists actually have to train their lazy, good-for-nothing left hands to do some pretty intricate stuff on the guitar neck. And look what they ask their highly trained, pen-wielding, snooker-cueing Ninja of a right hand to do: hold a plectrum and move it up and down. Big deal. Wouldn't it be a better idea to let the side of your body that's more readily adapted for delicate, co ordinated movements take over on the fretboard and give the other side of your brain a break?

I know of quite a few right-handed guitar players who think that we ought to hold the guitar the other way around, and I also know many left handers who've chosen to play as if right handed and have found that they have an advantage. My left-handed pupils who chose this path all made faster progress off the starting grid than their right-handed contemporaries, too, so it's definitely something worth considering before you get too far along the guitar-playing route.

One final word, though: there are some people who find it impossible even to consider anything other than a left-handed orientation with the guitar. If this is the case with you, and you've tried playing "right handed" with no success, feel free to ignore me and just go for it!

# first steps

OK, let's make a start. In order to make things as easy as possible, the first chords we're going to look at involve only two or three fingers and no stretches. Once again, don't worry about what the chords are called for now; at present, we just want to concentrate on making sure that everything's up and running.

**A7**

Just to recap on what the diagram above actually asks you to do, you need to place finger 1 on the second fret of the D string and finger 2 on the second fret of the B string. The little "x" over the bass E string is instructing you to leave out this note completely and play only the top five strings.

In order to make sure that everything's working properly, play the chord through one string at a time. This is the only way of finding out if there are any problems that need correcting. You might find a couple of things that need attention – for instance, the strings that you've got fingers on might sound muffled or buzzy and the G string might be a complete dud!

To correct the first problem, check out the position of

your thumb on your left hand – is it literally lying down on the job? The rule is "thumbs up", and it should definitely not be pointing toward the left. The position of the thumb is quite critical insofar that its job is to support the fingers while they go about their fretting business. Imagine you're holding a book in your left hand – your thumb would have to be opposite your fingers in order to offer some kind of counter-pressure. It's the same with the guitar – you don't need to grip the neck; you just need to maintain support for the fingers. If this isn't happening, your fingers will be pushing into space and won't have a hope of making the string sit against the fret firmly enough.

In other words, you'll probably have to do a bit of adjusting before you can expect results. Don't worry, though – it won't be too long before your hand remembers all of this information and chord playing feels absolutely natural.

As far as the problem with the muted G is concerned, prime suspects here are the fingers that fall on either side of it. Expect to find that one or other of your fingers is somehow overlapping its allotted space and touching the G slightly, effectively muting it. To cure this, you'll have to perform a little finger ballet to make sure that everything's clear. The first rule to observe is to make sure that your first and second fingers are touching the strings with their tips and not the fleshy pads, so stand 'em up on tiptoe for the best results.

Now let's look at another chord:

Once again, it's a two fingered chord employing only the first and second digits. Tackle this chord exactly as you did before, sounding each string one at a time, watching your thumb position, making sure that the string between your fingers (an open D this time) is sounding clearly and that your fingers are standing on tiptoe. Make any adjustments necessary and don't worry if everything feels awkward to begin with. Just think back to what it felt like the first few times you tried to ride a bicycle.

Now here's another chord to try:

This is another two-finger chord, and it has a very similar shape to the E7 we just looked at. All of the previous rules apply here, too.

Over the page is a review of your current practice routine. I've included a one-finger chord, too, just for good measure. This is all you'll need to look at to begin with. Remember, don't try to move too fast with your chords. Like I said, you'll need to allow time for muscles to stretch and develop, because this doesn't come overnight. Don't give in to impatience, either – we were all rookies once!

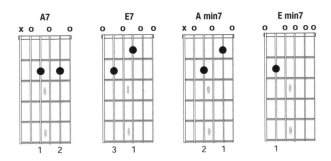

At first, don't spend any longer than about ten minutes running through these chords. You want to be able to pace yourself, and ten minutes is enough to begin with.

Expect some slight discomfort as your left hand begins to come to terms with actually having to work for a living, but anything more serious is a sign that something's not quite right. Pins and needles or fizziness in the hand or fingers shouldn't be ignored, and wrist pain is a sure sign that you should rest your hand. You've probably heard of RSI (Repetitive Strain Injury) and tendonitis, and you'll certainly want to avoid both of these ailments here. Take things slowly, give those muscles a chance to settle down and, as it says on all medicine bottles, if symptoms persist, seek medical advice.

# the right stuff

With any luck, you'll have found that things are beginning to get much easier and that you're getting a good, clean chord pretty much first time, every time. In a moment, we'll look at some three-finger chords, but now I'm just going to take a few moments to look at what your other hand should be doing.

On a basic level, there are two ways in which the right hand can sound the strings: the first, and probably most common, is by using a plectrum, and the second is by using the fingers. For the time being, I would advise that you use a plectrum, at least until you've got your chord-playing up and running. Then, if you decide that you want to play "fingerstyle", you can start down that road at a slightly later date.

Plectrums come in all shapes, sizes and materials, so it's a good idea to buy a few different varieties rather than several of the exact same sort. As a rough guide, you'll want something that feels comfortable to hold and use, and this judgement can really only be made over a period of time.

Plectrums, or *picks*, come in varying thicknesses, varying from about .44mm right up to 2mm or 3mm. Obviously, a .44mm plectrum is quite bendy, whereas anything approaching 1mm or more is really quite rigid. The degree of rigidity will have an effect on playing technique and is another area worth a little experimentation. Most rock guitarists go for quite thick plectrums, whereas many acoustic "strummers" tend to go for something much lighter altogether. It's a very personal thing, however, and there's no way that I could tell you which one would be exactly right for you – and the chances are that you won't know yourself until you've been playing for a while.

Once you've got yourself a fistful of plectrums, the next thing you'll need to do is learn how to hold one. They fit quite nicely between the right-hand index finger and thumb and should be held rather than gripped. Holding on too tight introduces a lot of tension into the right hand, which will have the effect of slowing you down. Try to let the other fingers of your right hand relax and try not to form a fist, as this is another source of instant unwanted tension.

Use only the very tip of the plectrum to play the strings. Anything more than 2-3mm of the pick and you're going in way too deep. You should think about applying a gentle stroke rather than attempting anything too heavy handed, as playing with too much of a swipe will result in your guitar producing a very unmusical sound

It'll take a while before you feel comfortable with a plectrum, and you'll probably become aware of a syndrome that has puzzled guitarists for years – just like there is a place where pens and pencils go to hide just when you need them, so do plectrums. I've found them in the hoover, in the washing machine and just about every other unlikely place you can name. On the bright side, if I can't find one, I always know there's a spare down the back of the sofa.

If you find it really awkward to get used to using a plectrum in the early stages, sounding the strings with your thumb is the next best thing. There really is so much to get used to when you start to play guitar that you can safely put off experimenting with plectrums for a little while longer.

# three-finger chords

We're working our way into chord playing via gradual steps, and now it's time to add another finger. Here's your first three-finger chord:

Looks remarkably similar to the E7 chord we looked at earlier, doesn't it? In some respects, all you're going to do is fill in the gap with your third finger, but the rules remain exactly the same as before: play only one note at a time to make sure that everything is ringing clear and then adjust where necessary. Here's another shape to try:

You might find that this particular shape bunches the fingers up to the extent that it's awkward to fit everything into its allotted space. Once again, it's just a question of making minor adjustments to the positions of your fingers and thumb until everything sounds right.

We're now going to take a look at a few more three-finger chord shapes. Take your time, apply the same rules as before and everything should be fine.

# stretching time

There are a number of chord shapes that call for your fingers to do a bit of stretching, and this is the next stage to tackle. Take a look at this chord shape:

**G major**

G major calls for you to place your second finger right over on the bass string while your third finger plays the top E string. It's going to feel very strange the first few times you try it, but stick with it and you'll soon have things up and running. Here are some more chords that all employ a bit of aerobics:

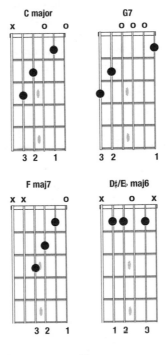

# four-finger chords

Obviously, the little finger on your left hand is the weakest of the bunch and will take quite a lot of training up before it becomes an effective member of your chord-playing squad. Like I said earlier, your left hand has a comparatively easy existence (if you're right handed), leaving all the really tough, intricate jobs to the right hand. Well, if you think about it, your left-hand little finger does practically nothing at all, and so playing the guitar comes as something of a serious wake-up call. In other words, to begin with, don't expect it to do anything that you ask of it. Practice will help lick it into shape, but it might be tough going in the initial stages.

Now let's look at our first four-finger shape:

We came across a very similar shape earlier, so hopefully your first, second and third fingers will feel in familiar surroundings, leaving you to concentrate on slotting in the new recruit at the third fret on the third string.

(Incidentally, if any of your fingers seem reluctant to find their allotted position on the fretboard, there's nothing wrong with reaching over with your right hand and literally putting the errant digit in its place. Just about everyone has a few problems with their fingers having a mind of their own in the initial stages. Things will improve very quickly, though, so don't give up!)

Time now for another chord shape:

This chord shape calls for fingers two, three and four to sit in a straight line at the second fret while finger one plays the note on the fourth string's first fret. It's a bit of a crush, and you'll need to apply quite a lot of adjustment before everything sounds dead right.

Here's a gallery of four-finger chords:

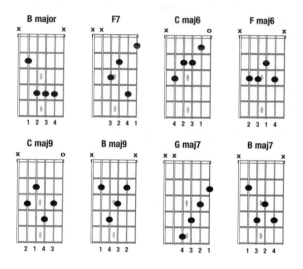

By now, you should have quite a lot of different chord shapes under your fingers and you should be nearly ready to take on the main section of this book, which details just about every chord you'll need for now. However, there's still one major thing we haven't considered: changing from one chord to another.

# all change

Someone asked me once if there was such a thing as an average number of chords that would appear in any given song. It wasn't something I'd really thought about too hard before, but the answer we came up with was four – that is, if the song concerned is a straightforward pop, rock or folk song. There are exceptions to every rule, of course – some jazz tunes can have a different chord on almost every beat, while other tunes can be quite content with only two – so it's an entirely fallible average, but I think that hearing this rule of thumb convinced the person who asked me that learning chords wasn't going to be too tough a ride.

Playing chords takes on a whole new meaning when you have to start changing from one to another, though. Getting the shape right is one thing, but swapping it with another presents a completely different set of riddles for the left hand.

In terms of rules regarding changing chords, I would say that there's a single golden one:

> Chord changes take place in midair,
> not on the fretboard

This doesn't mean that you're going to need a trapeze for this next bit, so if you don't have a head for heights, relax.

Many guitar fledglings tend to change between chords one finger at a time, and all this does is introduce a delay in whatever it is that's being played. Every time there's a chord change, you have to wait an extra couple of moments to allow the guitarist to adjust his fingers. So what's the correct way around?

Well, allow me to sidetrack for a few seconds here. You've probably seen computer-image morphing, where one picture turns smoothly into another – a dining table suddenly turns into a family car, for example, or a double-decker bus turns into a mountain range. It's all done with very clever computer programs by which the two different images are scanned in and the computer then crossfades one into the other, seamlessly and effectively. Well, that's what you've got to learn to do when you change chords, except that, instead of a computer, your brain will do nicely.

Look at these two chords:

**E major**

3 2 1

**A major**

1 2 3

You've met both of these chord shapes before, and by now you should feel quite comfortable playing both of them. If you want to change between them, however, you're presented with a fresh challenge. In music, chord changes happen "on the beat" – there's no time to make sure that each individual finger is in position. All of your fingers will have to change at once. With that in mind, I want you to try this experiment: play the E chord shown above, count up to four slowly and change the chord to A when you reach "four", like this:

E major / 1 / 2 / 3 / A major

Difficult, isn't it? Now take a good look at the two shapes individually and work out exactly what has to happen for one chord to "morph" into the next. In other words, you're doing exactly what a computer would do – you're scanning the two images and computing a seamless change between them. But this change has to happen at the precise moment that you release your hand from playing the E, and the only place that this can happen is in midair, while all fingers are off the fretboard. This is where the morph must take place so that, when your fingers hit the fretboard again to play the A, they're already in the right places.

Looking at chord changes in this way will save you an awful lot of grief in the future when you want to tighten up your rhythm playing. Then, when the shock realisation comes that chord changing has to be done using sleight of hand and not via the kind of fretboard choreography you might have allowed yourself to become used to, you won't have to undergo the trauma of wasting a lot of time correcting a bad habit.

After trying to morph between E and A, feel free to do likewise between all of the other chords we've looked at so far. This is also a good chance for you to put a simple practice routine in place to help you become familiar with some useful chord shapes and get used to changing between them.

Unfortunately, not every chord has its home down at the nut end of the guitar fretboard. You've probably seen guys and gals playing chords all over the guitar neck and might have begun to wonder how this fits in with what you've learned so far. In order to take this next step in your understanding of chords, we're going to have to look at a minute amount of music theory. Don't panic, I'm not going to try to teach you anything that you don't actually need to know!

# the musical alphabet

As you can see from taking a quick look at Section 2 of this book, there are three quite large families of chords: majors, minors and sevenths. I get asked the question "How many chords do I need to know?" quite often and generally give the reply, "At least 36." Here's how I worked that out.

In music, there are twelve notes, which go on repeating from the lowest note we can hear to the highest. It doesn't matter how long that takes; there are still only twelve notes. If you look at a piano keyboard, you'll see a whole line of notes that extend from very low grunty notes on the far left to high twinkly ones on the far right. There are around 88 keys on the piano but still only twelve notes. Each group of twelve is called an *octave*. The piano has about seven and a half octaves, while the guitar has only three and a half (although this varies between classical nylon-string, acoustic steel-string and electric models). So here is the musical alphabet written out:

| A | A♯/B♭ | B | C | C♯/D♭ | D | D♯/E♭ | E | F | F♯/G♭ | G | G♯/A♭ |
|---|-------|---|---|-------|---|-------|---|---|-------|---|-------|
| 1 | 2 | 3 | 4 | 5 | 6 | 7 | 8 | 9 | 10 | 11 | 12 |

You'll notice straight away that notes two, five, seven, ten and twelve all seem to have two names each. This is just one of music's funny little quirks. On a piano keyboard, these would be the black notes, and their position in the alphabet is related to the notes located on each side. Take note number two in the diagram above, for instance. It's known as both *A sharp* (to indicate its relationship to the A immediately before it) and *B flat* (indicating its relationship to the note that follows it). And so, as you've probably anticipated...

♯ = sharp
♭ = flat

While we're here, let's clear up a couple of frequently asked questions.

Q: *Why aren't there sharps and flats between every note?*

A: It's all to do with the way in which music evolved over the years. To simplify the answer grossly, the sharps and flats were a bit of an afterthought and had to be slotted in where they fitted.

Q: *Does it matter which name is used for one of these "dual-identity" notes?*

A: In general, using either isn't something for which you're going to be hounded down by the Music Police. There is a sort of etiquette in music that would recommend one or the other, depending on the circumstance in which it's going to be used, but everyone will know what you mean and that's the most important thing. The diagram over the page shows how the music alphabet – or *chromatic scale* – relates directly to the guitar.

So by now you should be able to work out how I arrived at the answer "36" a couple of paragraphs ago:

12 (notes in the scale) x 3 (types of chord) = 36

Knowing 36 chords will go a long way towards you having a chord for every common musical situation under your fingertips, and it would be true to say that

**E string**

The notes on the bass E string, proceeding up the neck, chromatically, from open E to the E at the 12th fret

you'll have covered quite a vast amount of territory with this fairly modest database. But, of course, it's not the end of the story. From this point, two factors come into play. The first is that there are different types of major, minor and seventh chords, most of which you'll meet in section two. This fact alone adds to the number of chords available for you to learn – although, of course, your basic stock of 36 are still by far the most common. The other factor relates back to something I mentioned before we took a look at the musical alphabet – the fact that there are chord shapes available all over the fretboard, which means that there are several locations in which you can play the basic 36. Add both of these factors together and you've got a good idea of why chord books always appear to be absolutely chock full. Let's do some more maths.

There are 36 basic chords and, on average, about five places on the guitar neck that you can play each of them, and so 36 x 5 = 180.

There are also about five different types of each chord, and so 5 x 180 = 900. (Learning chords is looking a bit more of a task now, isn't it? )

Of course, it won't help matters when I tell you that I've missed out a few. These are the chords that push on into the more rarefied areas of music like jazz, and despite the fact that I've detailed many of these in Section 2, I'm really talking about the more commonplace, mainstream types of chord for now.

The good news is that you can still reach a long way into music's innards with those basic 36 chords, so don't despair. I just wanted to give you a sense of breadth!

# moveable chords

So how exactly are we going to go about dealing with chords that don't sit quietly down at the nut end of the fretboard? Let's look at an example. And I think you're going to like this one.

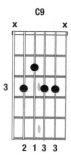

Before we do anything else, take a look at this:

Notice anything? Well, let's take a closer look at the diagrams. One thing to be aware of is the fact that both the top and bottom strings have got an "x" over them, meaning that you must be careful not to play these strings. You'll notice, too, that there is a number three by the first chord box and a five by the second. Apart from that, both diagrams tell you to put your fingers in exactly the same configuration. So what's going on? Welcome to one of the guitar's more convenient characteristics: the fact that a lot of the time you only have to learn one chord shape and then play it in twelve different places and you've got everything covered. These are known as *moveable chord shapes*, and they cut down on an awful lot of learning time. Suddenly, that frightening total of 900 chords doesn't look quite so daunting, does it? Well, not quite.

Of course, this is all very well, but how do you know where to play the chord shape once you've learned it? Look at a slightly enhanced version of a major-ninth chord over the page. You'll notice that the note on the fifth string has got an arrow pointing to it, with the word *root* nearby. The root is the note that gives the chord its name, and so, if you wanted to find a particular major-ninth chord, all you'd have to do would be to find its root on the fifth string and play

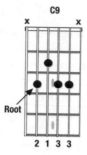

C9

x          x

Root

2 1 3 3

this particular shape. And the answer to your next questions is shown below:

A string

The notes on the A string. You can move the 9 chord to any of these roots and tell yourself that you've learned 12 chords

That's twelve chords from one shape. So wouldn't you be able to make quick work of learning those initial 36 chords if all you had to do was to learn one major shape, one minor shape and one seventh shape and just move them around? Well, there is a way that you can do just that. All you have to do is learn to play barre chords.

# barre chords

You might find yourself thinking, "Well, why don't I just learn a few of these barre chords right from the start and cut down on learning all those other shapes?" Just like life itself, things aren't that simple, and the main reason why this is so is that barre chords are actually quite difficult and rely on the left hand having developed a bit of muscle. For an example, look at this diagram:

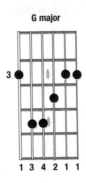

**G major**

1 3 4 2 1 1

If you've checked out the fingering underneath, you'll perhaps be asking yourself how your first finger can be in so many places at once. The answer is that the whole concept of barre chords means placing a finger across all six strings. It's usually your first finger, but beware that other permutations exist, although most of them involve the other fingers going only part of the way across. These are called *part barre chords* or *partial barres*.

Unless you've discovered hidden Herculean strength in your left hand overnight, you'll probably find that last example almost impossible – initially, at least. It's actually much better to work towards it in measured stages.

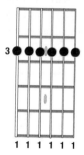

The shape above involves you placing your first finger over all six strings, but unlike the previous example you have no other finger to place, which makes the job a little more straightforward. With this particular shape (which isn't actually a chord, incidentally, more of an exercise), you apply exactly the same set of rules as you have in the past: sound one string at a time to make sure that you have a full set of notes. If not, suspect that your first finger isn't laying in the correct position. It should be very slightly on its side, in contact with the strings along the side that normally faces the thumb. To look at this another way, it means that the finger shouldn't be pressing "face down" flat on the fretboard but angled slightly to one side. It should also be snuggling up to the back of the fret like this:

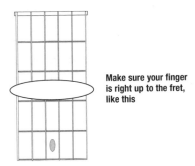

**Make sure your finger is right up to the fret, like this**

If things still aren't going well, remember to take a good look at your thumb position. It's absolutely vital that the thumb plays its role in supporting the first finger, so you might have to make quite a few adjustments before you can hear all six strings ringing clearly. One thing is for certain, though: it's not going to feel exactly normal to start with. You're asking your hand and finger to do something new, and it will take a while before things settle down. Those muscles are going to ache for a while, and it will be a little time before you can play too many barre chords in succession for too long because you'll lack the strength to do so.

My advice with barre chords is to take things slowly and break in your hand to its new task gradually. Don't overdo things. Remember what I said about avoiding RSI!

Once you've managed to get six clearly ringing notes from your barred first finger, try this next chord shape:

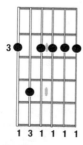

Nothing too strenuous here, just a barre with your third finger playing the fifth string. Nonetheless, it probably adds a new level of difficulty to the situation, so be patient while you get used to it.

Once you're fairly happy with the previous example, try adding another finger:

As this chord involves your little finger, which probably isn't quite up to full strength yet, you may find that this shape comes with yet another set of difficulties. If it really gives you nightmares, backtrack a little and keep practising the first two steps. The three Ps – patience, persistence and practice – generally win through!

Once you're playing the barred minor shape confidently, you can proceed to the next stage:

**G major**

1 3 4 2 1 1

Now all four fingers are employed and you've got a fully functioning major chord which is available to play all twelve majors in the pack. Now all that you need to know is which note gives the chord its name...

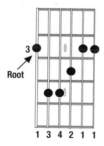

1 3 4 2 1 1

Skip back a few pages to where we looked at the notes on the E string and you'll have a handy guide to where exactly you can access all twelve major barre-chord shapes.

So now, all of the information you require from me is here:

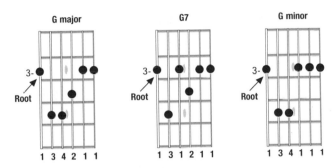

And you've got access to all 36 of the most important chords from three basic shapes. I would imagine that this sort of maths appeals to you as much as it does other guitar players who have trod this same path.

It gets better, too. Are you ready for another 36 chords? OK, then consider the three barre-chord shapes shown over the page. In exactly the same way as earlier, these chord shapes will allow you to access all of the major, minor and seventh shapes on the fifth string.

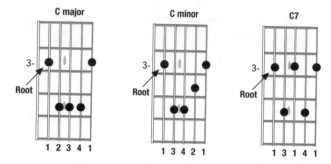

**Refer back to the diagram
on page 54 showing notes
on the A string to access all
major, minor and 7th barres**

## summary

Now that you know how to read chord boxes, you've
played quite a few "nut-position" chords and you
understand moveable- and barre-chord shapes, you're
ready for Section 2. But if you're fascinated about how
chords get their names, you might want to read the
next chapter first. Good luck!

# what are chords?

As far as we know, music has existed in one form or another almost as long as man himself has. We can't really guess at what very early music sounded like, because it was only comparatively recently that anyone started to write it down in such a way that it could be universally understood (that is, if you call 300-400 years ago recent). Nobody can be really sure when the first chord showed up in the archaeology of music, either. Exactly what it was or how it came about is lost in the murkiness of speculation. It was all part of music evolving naturally, until eventually it became commonplace for melodies to be supported by chords and music began to sound more like it does today.

So a chord is really just more than one note played at once? Well, just about. A music-dictionary definition would tell us that a chord is actually more than two notes at once (two notes played together is known as a *diad*), but now you've come across that word, I'd advise you to forget it again, unless you want to slip it in at your next dinner party.

# what chords do

Basically, the job of a chord is to support a melody line, in much the same way that a post supports a fence. This is true irrespective of the style of music. Whether it's orchestral, rock, pop or country, chords and melody have exactly the same sort of relationship. They're basically the same sort of chords, too. A lot of people think that the chords played by an orchestra must be somehow different from those found in other types of music, but that's not the case. Believe it or not, the chords played in a symphony contain the same number of notes as those that would be used to accompany a pop song. The biggest difference is the way in which they sound – and that's all. For instance, if you spread a chord so that violins are playing one note, violas and cellos are playing another note and the basses are playing another, it's going to sound very full, and yet you've still only used three notes! You could play exactly the same notes together on your guitar and get the same chord. It might not sound quite as grand as it would when played by a string section, but it's essentially exactly the same.

# how chords get their names

Chords are drawn from scales, the same building blocks that make up melody. There are lots of different types of chord, each with different shorthand-style names – so many, in fact, that trying to understand exactly which one fits where and why is quite perplexing. But if we take a musical scale in letter form and look at it more closely, it's easier to see where the individual chord names actually come from.

Here's a C major scale:

$$
\begin{array}{cccccccc}
C & D & E & F & G & A & B & C \\
1 & 2 & 3 & 4 & 5 & 6 & 7 & 1
\end{array}
$$

As you can see from the numbers underneath, there are seven notes in the scale, and the simplest chord we can form from them uses the first, third and fifth: C, E and G. When we sound these particular notes together, we end up with the chord of C major, just like the one we saw on page 16.

C major

As you can see from the chord box on the previous page, the only notes we're playing are C, E and G, despite the fact that it's a five-string chord. If you look at another version of C major, you can see that, once again, it's the same three notes being used:

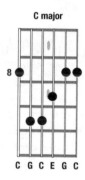

**C major**

C G C E G C

These all-important three notes are known as a *triad* and form the basis for all of the other chords taken from the scale. For instance, if you add the sixth note of the scale, take a look at what happens.

C D E F G A B C
1 2 3 4 5 6 7 1

The sixth note in the C scale is an A, and so, if you add it to the basic triad, you end up with this formula...

C E G A
1 3 5 6

...and this chord shape.

It's still a C major chord. All that's happened is that we've added another note from the scale in order to bring out a different set of characteristics – a different shade or flavour, if you like.

We call the chord C major sixth (or sometimes just plain C6) as a shorthand version of the chord formula. What "C major sixth" actually means is "the basic triad plus the C major scale's sixth note". This description can be extended to apply to every other chord symbol; they are all abbreviations.

Of course, this naming convention applies to chords from other scales, too. Let's look at a minor scale:

$$\begin{array}{cccccccc} C & D & E\flat & F & G & A\flat & B\flat & C \\ 1 & 2 & 3 & 4 & 5 & 6 & 7 & 1 \end{array}$$

This a scale of C minor, and if we take the first, third and fifth notes, we end up with the minor triad or basic minor chord.

$$\begin{array}{ccc} C & E\flat & G \\ 1 & 3 & 5 \end{array}$$

This particular chord would look like this on the fretboard:

**C minor**

C E♭ G C

Again, you can see that only the three notes from the triad have been used. Here's another shape for C minor:

**C minor**

C G C E♭ E

It's still the same notes as before, although the way they're mixed is slightly different.

If we wanted to explore other minor chords, we'd find the same kind of shorthand naming system as before. Look at the formula for C minor7:

$$C \quad E♭ \quad G \quad B♭$$
$$1 \quad 3 \quad 5 \quad 7$$

The chord name tells us that it's a C minor triad with the seventh note from the scale added to it, but in a much more convenient format.

One word of caution here about the minor scale: unlike its major counterpart, the minor scale is available in more than one form. There are natural-minor, melodic-minor and harmonic-minor scales in music and chords are built from a cross-section of all three. Don't let this worry you too much, though; it's not going to affect the chord-playing side of your guitarmanship!

In order to make the system of naming chords absolutely transparent, let's take a look at another example. This version is known as the *dominant* (or *seventh*) scale:

C D E F G A B♭ C
1 2 3 4 5 6 7 1

As you can see, the basic triad is exactly the same as the one for the major scale. Chords based on the dominant scale only really assume their true musical identities when we include the seventh note.

C E G B♭
1 3 5 7

This chord is called C7, and here's how it appears on the fretboard:

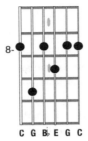

C G B♭ E G C

And here's another version, just so you can double check:

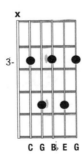

C G B♭ E G

# seven up

You might have noticed that some chord names contain numbers greater than seven, and as there are only seven notes to choose from in the scale, you might be wondering how this can be. But take a look at the following:

| C | D | E | F | G | A | B | C | D | E | F | G | A | B | C |
|---|---|---|---|---|---|---|---|---|---|----|---|----|---|---|
| 1 | 2 | 3 | 4 | 5 | 6 | 7 | 1 | 9 | 3 | 11 | 5 | 13 | 7 | 1 |

This represents one of music's older traditions, whereby chord naming is extended over two octaves of a scale, literally two scales laid end to end. When this happens, the original triad retains its identity. If you look above, you'll notice that the one, three and five are represented in the second octave. The seventh also manages to keep its original number, too, and so the newcomers to the chord-naming game are nine, eleven and 13. So a C9 chord formula would look like this:

| C | E | G | B♭ | D |
|---|---|---|----|---|
| 1 | 3 | 5 | 7  | 9 |

And a C13...

| C | E | G | B♭ | D | A  |
|---|---|---|----|---|----|
| 1 | 3 | 5 | 7  | 9 | 13 |

Sometimes you'll see chord titles like this one...

C7♭9

...and wonder exactly what's going on. Of course,

again this is shorthand. Look at the chord formula for
the chord of C7♭9.

$$\begin{array}{ccccc} C & E & G & B♭ & D♭ \\ 1 & 3 & 5 & 7 & ♭9 \end{array}$$

Sometimes notes from outside the scale turn up in
chords, and if this is the case then the chord name will
inform you of this by telling you which note or notes
are affected. In the case of the chord above, the ninth
has been *flattened* – instead of a D, the note required
is a D♭. This little group of chords are known as *altered
chords* and crop up from time to time, usually to
introduce a little dissonance.

This system of naming chords is hundreds of years old
(it might have been based on an original Greek system
for naming notes, which is even older), so you can't
expect it to be too logical. The best thing to do is to
accept it at face value. At least now you know where
chords get their names from!

# care for a trim, sir?

I've got one final point to make before you can
consider yourself well grounded in all matters of chord
lore. The guitar has only six strings and yet some

chords call for more notes than we can play at once. In these cases, guitar chords tend to be trimmed a little. Therefore, don't be surprised if you see a chord that doesn't contain all of the notes that are shown in its basic recipe. It's just been cut to fit, that's all.

# family groups

We've just met the three main chord families in music: majors, minors and sevenths. Basically, it would be true to say that all of the chords you'll ever need fit into one of these groups or another, so in this book I'll be looking at them one at a time.

Along the way, you should meet all of the chords that you need to take you virtually anywhere you want to go with music. Some are more common than others; some are harder to play than others. Just remember that your fingers have probably still got a lot of settling in to do and so, if you find a particular fingering really difficult, spend some time practising it. Be prepared to re-evaluate the positioning of your fingers and thumb and all will be well.

# section two

# a dictionary
# of chords

For the examples in this book, I've tried to come up with the easiest and most practicable versions of all of the chords shown. However, owing to the way in which the guitar is tuned, some of these chords are more difficult than others. Just a quick flick through will probably tell you why certain keys in music are more guitar-friendly than others!

A by-product of this means that many guitar-orientated songs use relatively easy chords, which is good news because the chances are that you won't encounter any of the more awkward chord shapes in your initial foray into music. So don't worry if chords like D♭ major seem difficult or even impossible at first; the chances are that, by the time you need them, your fingers will have strengthened to the point at which it's no longer a problem. As your skills develop, you'll perhaps want to become more adventurous and tackle some of the more difficult fingerings as you come across them.

# yoga for guitarists

At first your fingers won't be very flexible, and to begin with some of the left-hand finger positions will seem impossible. For instance, you'll find fingerings which require your third finger to extend across three strings in the form of a partial barre, and it will take a while before things have loosened up enough for this to happen easily. It's something like yoga – in the end, your fingertips will attain a lot more capacity for movement than they have in the initial stages and even the awkward fingerings will cause you no trouble at all. The more you attempt these tricky chord voicings, the easier they will become. Just think of your initial attempts as a work in progress!

# the major family

## C

### C barre versions

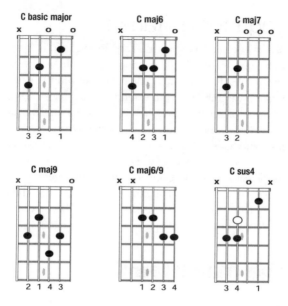

Note: "Sus" (suspended) chords are usually followed immediately by a straight major chord. In the chord positions that follow, I have outlined the note that will change the sus chord back to a major in white.

# C#/Db

### C#/Db barre versions

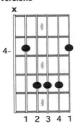

9-  1 3 4 2 1 1

x
4-  1 2 3 4 1

### C#/Db basic major

x
4 3 1 2 1

### C#/Db maj6

x        x
4 2 3 1

### C#/Db maj7

x
4 3 1 1 1

### C#/Db maj9

x        x
2 1 4 3

### C#/Db maj6/9

x   x
1 2 3 4

### C#/Db sus4

x  x
4-
2 3 4 1

# D

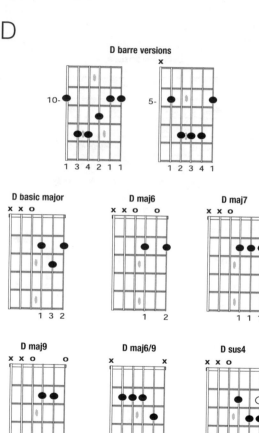

**D barre versions**

**D basic major**

**D maj6**

**D maj7**

**D maj9**

**D maj6/9**

**D sus4**

# D#/E♭

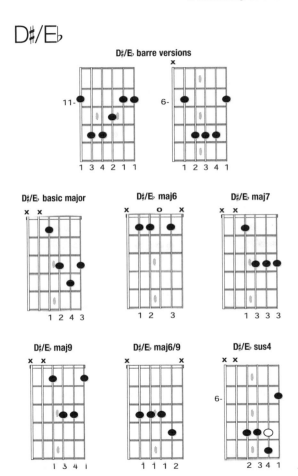

**D#/E♭ barre versions**

11-   ·   ·

x

6-

1 3 4 2 1 1          1 2 3 4 1

**D#/E♭ basic major**

1 2 4 3

**D#/E♭ maj6**

1 2   3

**D#/E♭ maj7**

1 3 3 3

**D#/E♭ maj9**

1 3 4 1

**D#/E♭ maj6/9**

1 1 1 2

**D#/E♭ sus4**

6-

2 3 4 1

# E

## E barre versions

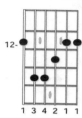

## E basic major

## E maj6

## E maj7

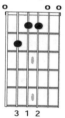

## E maj9

## E maj6/9

## E sus4

# F

### F barre versions

### F basic major

### F maj6

### F maj7

### F maj9

### F maj6/9

### F sus4

# F#/Gb

## F#/Gb barre versions

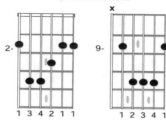

## F#/Gb basic major

## F#/Gb maj6

## F#/Gb maj7

## F#/Gb maj9

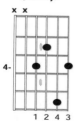

## F#/Gb maj6/9

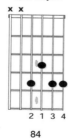

## F#/Gb sus4

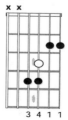

# G

### G barre versions

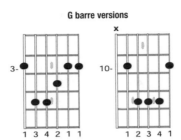

### G basic major

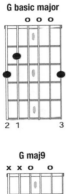

### G maj6

### G maj7

### G maj9

### G maj6/9

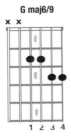

### G sus4

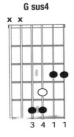

# G#/A♭

## G#/A♭ barre versions

## G#/A♭ basic major

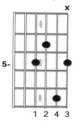

## G#/A♭ maj6

## G#/A♭ maj7

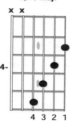

## G#/A♭ maj9

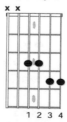

## G#/A♭ maj6/9

## G#/A♭ sus4

# A

**A barre versions**

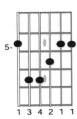
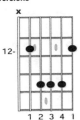

**A basic major**

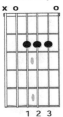

**A maj6**

**A maj7**

**A maj9**

**A maj6/9**

**A sus4**

# A♯/B♭

## A♯/B♭ barre versions

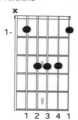

## A♯/B♭ basic major

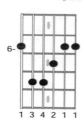

## A♯/B♭ maj6

## A♯/B♭ maj7

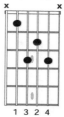

## A♯/B♭ maj9

## A♯/B♭ maj6/9

## A♯/B♭ sus4

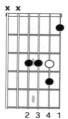

# B

## B barre versions

## B basic major

1 2 3 4

## B maj6

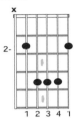

3 1 2

## B maj7

1 3 2 4

## B maj9

1 4 3 2

## B maj6/9

2 1 3

## B sus4

2 3 4 1

89

# the minor family

## C

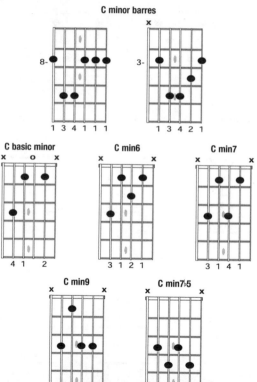

**C minor barres**

**C basic minor**   **C min6**   **C min7**

**C min9**   **C min7♭5**

# C#/Db

### C#/Db minor barres

### C#/Db basic minor

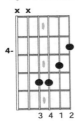

### C#/Db min6

### C#/Db min7

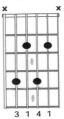

### C#/Db min9

### C#/Db min7b5

# D

## D minor barres

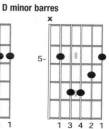

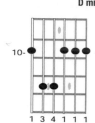

## D basic minor

## D min6

## D min7

## D min9

## D min7♭5

# D#/E♭

### D#/E♭ minor barres

11-

1 3 4 1 1 1

x

6-

1 3 4 2 1

### D#/E♭ basic minor

x x

1 3 4 2

### D#/E♭ min6

x x

1 3 1 2

### D#/E♭ min7

x x

1 4 2 3

### D#/E♭ min9

x      x

6-

? 1 3 4

### D#/E♭ min7♭5

x x

1 3 3 3

# E

### E minor barres

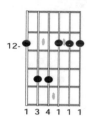

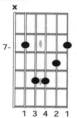

12-

1 3 4 1 1 1

7-

1 3 4 2 1

### E basic minor

1 2

### E min6

1 2 3

### E min7

1

### E min9

1 2

### E min7♭5

1 3 3 3

94

# F

### F minor barres

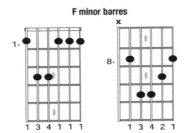

### F basic minor

### F min6

### F min7

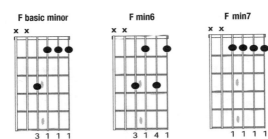

### F min9

### F min7♭5

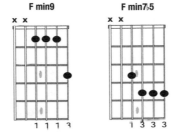

# F♯/G♭

### F♯/G♭ minor barres

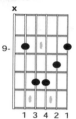

2-

1 3 4 1 1 1

x

9-

1 3 4 2 1

### F♯/G♭ basic minor

x x

3 1 1 1

### F♯/G♭ min6

x x

3 1 4 1

### F♯/G♭ min7

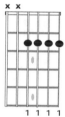

x x

1 1 1 1

### F♯/G♭ min9

x x

1 1 1 3

### F♯/G♭ min7♭5

x x

1 3 3 3

# G

## G minor barres

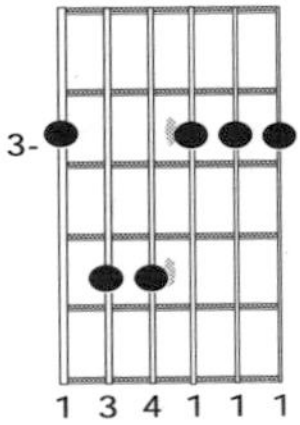

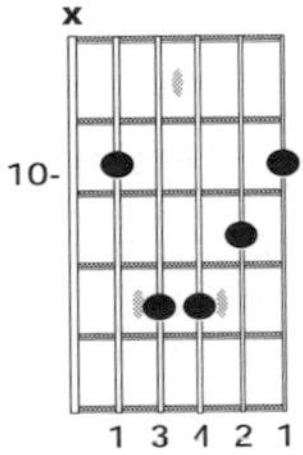

3-

x

10-

1 3 4 1 1 1

1 3 4 2 1

## G basic minor

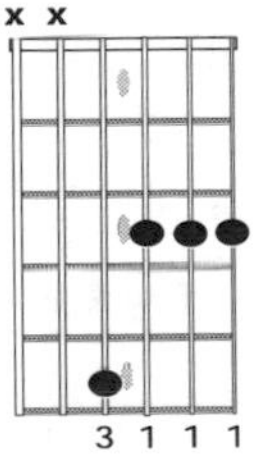

x x

3 1 1 1

## G min6

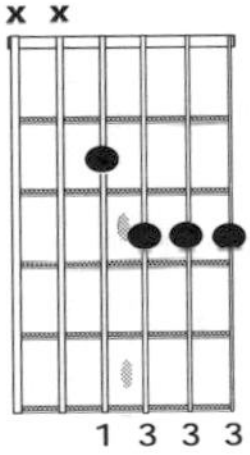

x x

1 3 3 3

## G min7

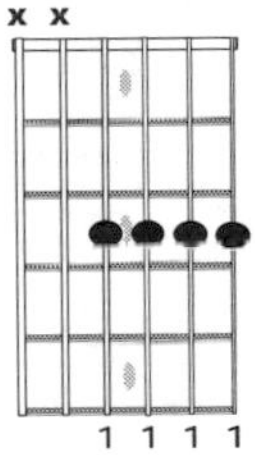

x x

1 1 1 1

## G min9

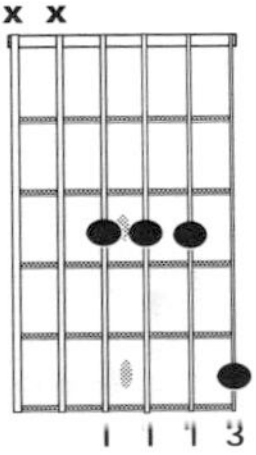

x x

1 1 1 3

## G min7♭5

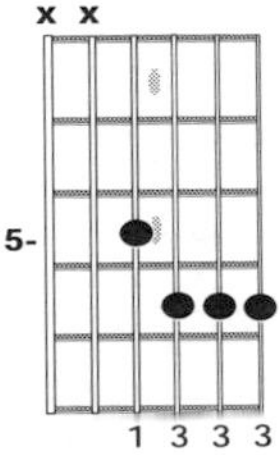

x x

5-

1 3 3 3

97

# G#/A♭

### G#/A♭ minor barres

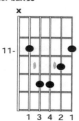

### G#/A♭ basic minor

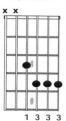

### G#/A♭ min6

### G#/A♭ min7

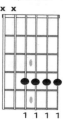

### G#/A♭ min9

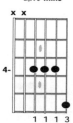

### G#/A♭ min7♭5

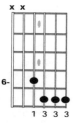

# A

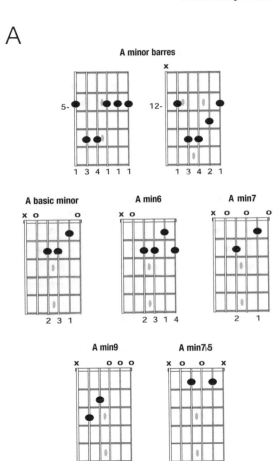

**A minor barres**

**A basic minor**

**A min6**

**A min7**

**A min9**

**A min7♭5**

# A#/B♭

### A#/B♭ minor barres

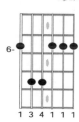

6-

1 3 4 1 1 1

x

1-

1 3 4 2 1

### A#/B♭ basic minor

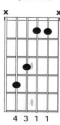

x x

3 4 2 1

### A#/B♭ min6

x x

2 3 1 4

### A#/B♭ min7

x x

3 1 2 1

### A#/B♭ min9

x x

4 3 1 1

### A#/B♭ min7♭5

x x

1 3 2 4

100

# B

## B minor barres

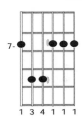

7-

2-

1 3 4 1 1 1

1 3 4 2 1

## B basic minor

3 4 2 1

## B min6

2 3 1 4

## B min7

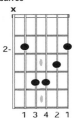

3 1 2 1

## B min9

1   2 3

## B min7♭5

1 3 2 4

# the dominant family

C

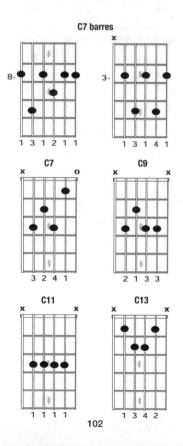

C7 barres

C7

C9

C11

C13

102

# C#/D♭

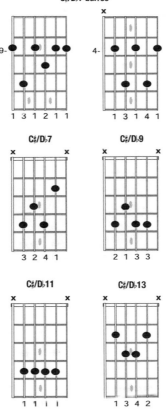

**C#/D♭7 barres**

9-          1 3 1 2 1 1

4-          1 3 1 4 1

**C#/D♭7**            **C#/D♭9**

3 2 4 1        2 1 3 3

**C#/D♭11**          **C#/D♭13**

1 1 1 1        1 3 4 2

103

# D

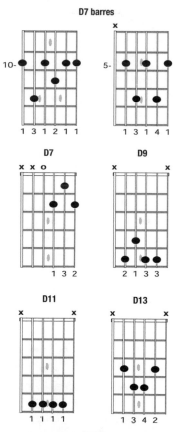

**D7 barres**

**D7**   **D9**

**D11**   **D13**

# D♯/E♭

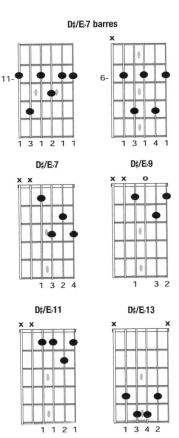

D♯/E♭7 barres

D♯/E♭7

D♯/E♭9

D♯/E♭11

D♯/E♭13

# E

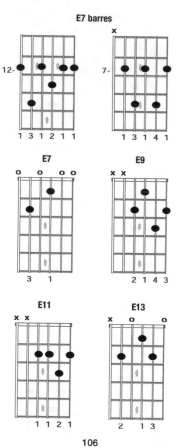

# F

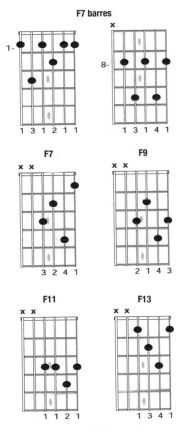

**F7 barres**

**F7**   **F9**

**F11**   **F13**

# F#/Gb

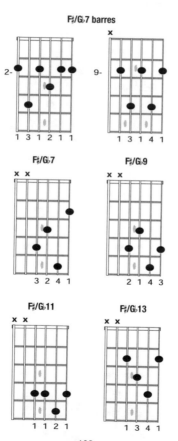

**F#/Gb7 barres**

**F#/Gb7**

**F#/Gb9**

**F#/Gb11**

**F#/Gb13**

# G

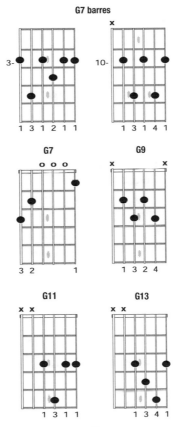

**G7 barres**

**G7**

**G9**

**G11**

**G13**

# G#/A♭

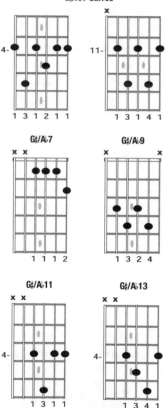

G#/A♭7 barres

G#/A♭7

G#/A♭9

G#/A♭11

G#/A♭13

# A

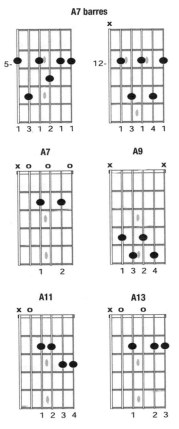

**A7 barres**

**A7**  **A9**

**A11**  **A13**

# A#/B♭

### A#/B♭7 barres

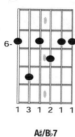

6-

1 3 1 2 1 1

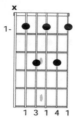

x

1-

1 3 1 4 1

### A#/B♭7

x x

1 1 1 2

### A#/B♭9

x x o

1 3 3 3

### A#/B♭11

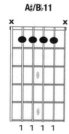

x x

1 1 1 1

### A#/B♭13

x x

2 1 3 4

# B

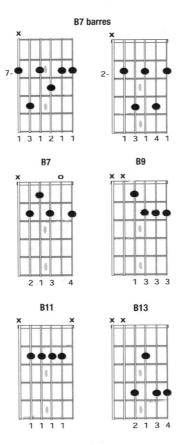

**B7 barres**

**B7**  **B9**

**B11**  **B13**

# altered-seventh chords

C

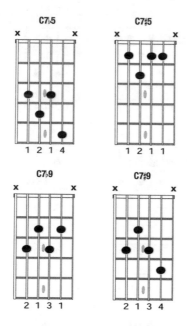

There are many more altered-seventh chords available than the selection shown here. I've concentrated on the more common types that you're likely to encounter – for instance, the 7♯9 series are almost indispensable when it comes to playing blues. This selection will serve as a good grounding in the altered-dominant series and should form a solid foundation on which to build further study.

# C♯/D♭

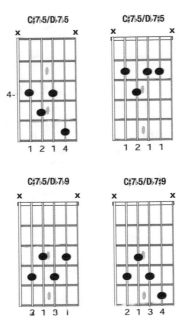

# D

**D7♭5**

**D7♯5**

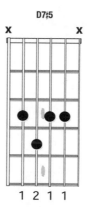

**D7♭9**

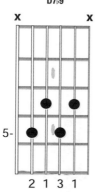

**D7♯9**

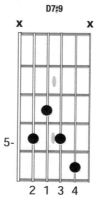

# D♯/E♭

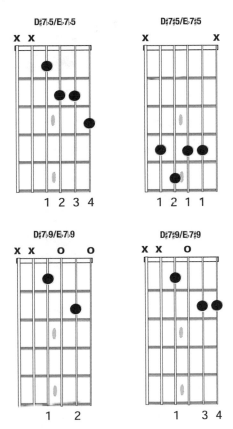

D♯7♭5/E♭7♭5

D♯7♯5/E♭7♯5

D♯7♭9/E♭7♭9

D♯7♯9/E♭7♯9

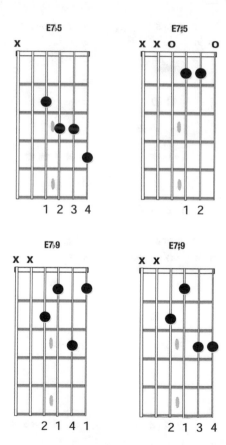

# E

# F

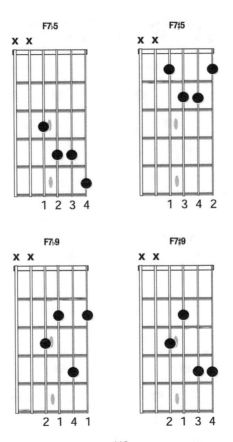

F7♭5

F7♯5

F7♭9

F7♯9

# F♯/G♭

### F♯7♭5/G♭7♭5

2 4 1 3

### F♯7♯5/G♭7♯5

1 3 4 2

### F♯7♭9/G♭7♭9

2 1 4 1

### F♯7♯9/G♭7♯9

2 1 3 4

# G

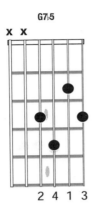

G7♭5

G7♯5

G7♭9

G7♯9

# G#/A♭

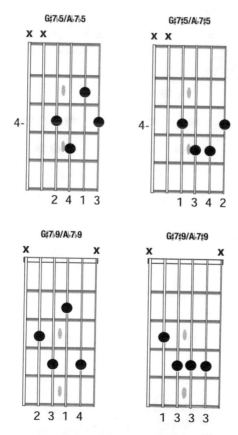

G#7♭5/A♭7♭5

G#7#5/A♭7#5

G#7♭9/A♭7♭9

G#7#9/A♭7#9

# A

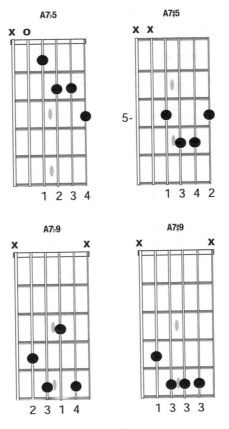

# A♯/B♭

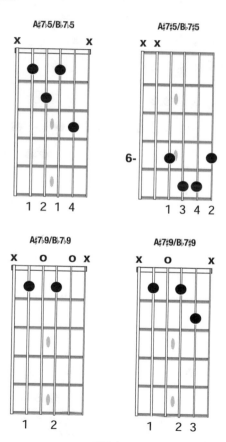

A♯7♭5/B♭7♭5

x          x

1 2 1 4

A♯7♯5/B♭7♯5

x x

6-

1 3 4 2

A♯7♭9/B♭7♭9

x   o   o x

1       2

A♯7♯9/B♭7♯9

x   o       x

1   2 3

# B

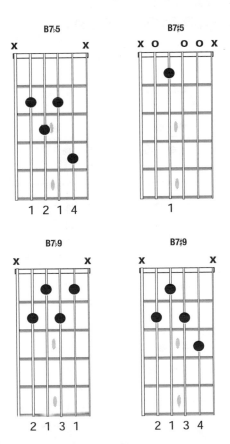

B7♭5

B7♯5

B7♭9

B7♯9

# diminished and augmented chords

## C

## C#/Db

# D

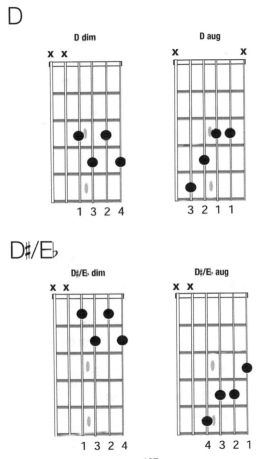

D dim

D aug

# D♯/E♭

D♯/E♭ dim

D♯/E♭ aug

# E

**E dim**

X X

1 3 2 4

**E aug**

X X

3 2 1 1

# F

**F dim**

X X

1 3 2 4

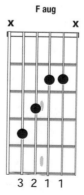

**F aug**

X X

3 2 1 1

# F♯/G♭

### F♯/G♭ dim

### F♯/G♭ aug

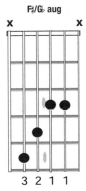

# G

### G dim

### G aug

# G#/A♭

### G#/A♭ dim

x x

1 3 2 4

### G#/A♭ aug

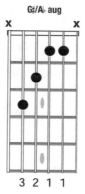

x x

3 2 1 1

# A

### A dim

x x

1 3 2 4

### A aug

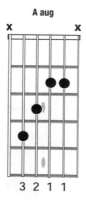

x x

3 2 1 1

# A♯/B♭

### A♯/B♭ dim

### A♯/B♭ aug

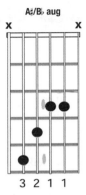

# B

### B dim

### B aug

# guitar strings

Once upon a time, a long time ago, I used to work in a music shop. We've all done it at one time or another. It's basically a case of satisfying the need to get some kind of job in the music business that will pay the rent while we hatch our master plan to become the next Joni Mitchell, or whoever.

So I've seen music-shop life from both sides now and reckon that I'm fairly familiar with most things that go on in the guitar-accessory-purchasing arena.

One thing that used to bring guitar "newbies" close to a nervous breakdown was buying new guitar strings. It seems simple enough, after all – all you want is a brand-new pack of shiny guitar strings to replace the filth-encrusted, rusty slivers of steel that currently inhabit your treasured instrument – but few are quite ready for the barrage of options the simple request "Can I have a new set of strings, please?" can produce. "What gauge?" "Which brand?" "Acoustic or electric?" "Nickel-steel or…?" The inquisition can be relentless, grinding on until the hapless guitar novice has to admit that he is well out of his depth and looks around, hoping that some kindly soul will throw him a line lest the fathomless pit of guitar-shop treachery swallow him whole.

Now, I take some pride in the fact that I was always The Most Helpful Person On Earth when I ruled the music shop in which I worked. In fact, I probably hold the record for convincing people to shop elsewhere because we didn't have something that I knew my customer needed. All treaties from the shop management to "sell them something we have in stock and don't send them away empty handed" fell on these deaf ears. I lasted only three months. Still, I'm sure that that puts me up alongside Florence Nightingale in terms of selflessly serving a cause.

So let's have a look at how you go about playing the new-strings game to the extent that you can leave the guitar shop in question with your pride intact, holding a set of strings that is exactly right for you.

# what gauge?

Guitar strings come in a wide variety of gauges. That is to say that they're available in many different thicknesses, measured in thousandths of an inch. As far as electric strings are concerned (see below for the differences in gauges between acoustic and electric strings), the "default" gauge is .009-.042. You'll hear guitarists standing around in clutches proclaiming that, when it comes to guitar strings, they "use nines". This is shorthand for saying that their strings measure up something like this:

$$E = .009$$
$$B = .011$$
$$G = .016$$
$$D = .024$$
$$A = .032$$
$$E = .042$$

Of course, this being far from a perfect world, expect to find minute changes creeping into this standard format from manufacturer to manufacturer. More on them later...

In any case, a set of .009s is most likely the set of default strings that was fitted onto your electric guitar when you bought it, and if you're getting along with them fine at present then there's not really any real reason to rock the boat by changing things around just yet.

Guitarists become string aficionados by degrees, you see, and if it's still early days for you in the guitar trenches, then it's really good advice to stick to what you know. Later on, you might decide that you want to experiment with string gauges, but it's really best to leave things be until you gain more experience. One of the main reasons for this is that, if you change your string gauge on a whim, it can upset things on your guitar and actually make it harder for you to play. In fact, if your guitar has a tremolo unit, like a Fender Stratocaster or some kind of derivative, you could be landing yourself in a whole new world of pain by switching gauges, so beware. (The full, ghastly facts are disclosed in Chapter 6, to be read only if you have a strong stomach.)

# for your eyes only

For now, we'll take a whistle-stop tour around the string-gauge lot. Just tell yourself that this is information you can use at some point in your playing future, although not quite yet.

The lightest (ie thinnest) gauge commercially available are "eights" – that is, the top E string in this particular set clocks in at a featherweight .008. And before you begin mumbling to yourself that a thousandth of an inch can't make that much difference, let me tell you here and now that yes, it can!

$$E = .008$$
$$B = .011$$
$$G = .014$$
$$D = .022$$
$$A = .030$$
$$E = .038$$

I know of only one player who can make a set of eights work: Queen's Brian May. In order to get the best from a set of strings this slight, you need an almost impossibly light touch, and it's not recommended that you experiment. I'm only mentioning them here because they actually exist!

All other string gauges go up from .009 on the top string in measured stages. Next along the line is, not surprisingly, .010s, or "tens".

$$E = .010$$
$$B = .013$$
$$G = .017$$
$$D = .026$$
$$A = .036$$
$$E = .046$$

Once again, things might look like they haven't changed too radically, but you'd be surprised by how different a set of tens feels if you've become used to using nines.

Moving up from tens, we have .011s, or "elevens", which report for duty like this:

E = .011
B = .014
G = .018
D = .028
A = .038
E = .048

After this, we reach the real heavyweights:

E = .012
B = .016
G = .024 (wound)
D = .032
A = .042
E = .052

The first real difference you'll see with a set of twelves is that the G string is actually wound, just like your D, A and E strings are in lighter gauges. The reason for this is all tied up with physics and confounds any attempts to offer a simple explanation. The best I can do is say that you can't get a string to stay in tune at this level of thickness without it being wound.

If you're really curious about the exact, scientific reasoning behind this phenomenon, I'm sure that some diligent savant has pinned it up on the internet somewhere. For the rest of you, I'd advise you to walk away slowly and leave them to it.

A set of .012s should never be taken lightly. Try bending strings on these babies and your fingertips will shred, blister, bleed, threaten to leave home and more besides. Your guitar will probably want a few quiet words with you, too...

Theoretically, of course, you could go on increasing string gauges until you reach something that wouldn't look out of place on a suspension bridge, but good old practicability calls a halt at around .012s, or maybe .013s in times of war.

Having said all that, of course, there are always exceptions, such as people who enjoy pain, mavericks and, in this case, Australians – the champion of heavy strings is Aussie slide player Dave Hole, who uses (gulp) a .015 as a top E. But Dave's a slide player, and they're all a little weird. Remember that being a slide player means that you're protected from the outrages that strings can otherwise inflict on soft skin tissue by a healthy lump of brass tubing.

## hybrids

As string manufactures became ever more eager to appease the quirkiness of jobbing guitarists everywhere, a new breed of string gauge came on to the market. These became known as *hybrid sets*, which, translated from argot into plain English, means that you end up with "light top, heavy bottom" types of variation (or vice versa) across the range. So, instead of the more regular .009-.042, for instance, you can get .009-.046, as below:

$$E = .009$$
$$B = .011$$
$$G = .016$$
$$D = .026$$
$$A = .036$$
$$E = .046$$

Other variations abound. Ask a dozen or so top

professionals what their preferences are for strings and you're likely to come up with a dozen different answers. But, as I said earlier, it takes time to become a connoisseur, and you can bet that all of these guys have been in the guitar-playing business for so long that they've had all the time necessary to become picky and choosy.

# so why use heavy strings?

There are many reasons why different players choose the heavy path of guitar string enlightenment. For instance, a lot of players who start out on acoustic guitar – on which string gauges are traditionally heavier than on their electric counterparts – might want to retain something of the feel of their acoustic when they switch over.

Jazz players often fall into this category. Jazz guitar started life on acoustic guitar – the electric guitar was used really a means of being heard rather than for any other reason – and so jazz players tend to use more acoustic-friendly strings on their beloved archtop electrics (ie those big old buggers with f-holes).

Born-and-bred electric players sometimes migrate to heavy gauges because they recognise the fact that their tone is improved by doing so. Volume is increased, too. When you think about it, thicker strings represent more metal vibrating in the guitar pick-up's magnetic field, which produces more electric current, which in turn means more volume from the guitar.

Getting back to the guitar-shop game, the next question you'll need answers for is...

# which brand?

Just like soap powder and toothpaste, there are a large number of guitar-string brand names to chose between. They all seem to do the same basic job, however – and you can bet they all insist that their product does it the best! Usually, players tend to settle for one particular brand for the same reason that they'd chose any brand name over another: habit, product reliability and so on.

In my own case, I stuck to one brand of strings for years because once, just before a gig, I changed my strings, tuned them up to pitch, put my guitar in its case and then into the boot of my car, drove to a gig in the freezing cold, went into a warm concert hall and the guitar was still perfectly in tune. I was so impressed that I was loyal to that brand for a long time afterwards!

The truth of the matter is that there is actually very little to choose between, as far as the many different makes of string are concerned. There are relatively few actual string-manufacturing plants spread across the planet but loads and loads of brand names. You work it out.

All I can say is, as with many other items in the marketplace, if you buy cheap, you'll regret it. You don't have to pick the most expensive brand; something around the mid to upper-mid price range should do the job nicely. Cheap strings, however, won't stay in tune and tend to break more easily.

Basically, it's a buyer's market. There are plenty of manufacturers out there, all wanting your custom. Experiment a bit and you'll find that you settle on one particular brand and gauge and then stick with them for years.

# acoustic or electric?

This might seem to be not even worth mentioning. Obviously, if you've got an electric guitar, you'll be wanting electric guitar strings and if you've got an acoustic... I guess you can probably work out the rest of that particular equation for yourself. I only mention it here because it gives rise to a sub-question:

# what's the difference?

In short, electric-guitar strings won't sound right on an acoustic guitar, and vice versa. The main difference has everything to do with the wound strings, as opposed to the good old plain steel "top" strings. To put it plainly, the phosphor bronze wrapped strings for acoustic guitar won't get your electric guitar's pick-ups very excited at all, whereas nickel-wound steel will give the optimum electromagnetic response.

There's nothing stopping you from putting electric strings on an acoustic, but they will sound reedy and thin if you do, owing to the difference in materials used in the manufacturing process. Which brings us neatly to the next question:

# nickel-steel or...?

Originally, guitar strings were said to be made from catgut, but before you start eyeing up the moggy with malicious intent let me tell you that it was more likely that this referred to sheep intestine than the local ginger tom. Why it got the name "catgut" in the first place is a mystery; it probably just sounded better than "sheepgut". Perhaps it was just to keep the local cat population in its place

In any case, since then, gut strings have been replaced by man-made and far more animal-friendly nylon, and metal strings for guitars and many other kinds of stringed instruments are now pretty much the norm.

As far as materials and actual manufacturing processes are concerned, a lot of research has been undertaken in the interest of bringing you and me a better guitar string. Various innovative processes have been tacked onto the basic steel-wire standard over the years. We've seen different types of core used for wound strings (basically wraps of steel or bronze around a metal core), we've seen cryogenically frozen strings (seriously), hand-made strings, Gore-Tex-wrapped strings and many other wonders of the modern string world. A few of them have some sort of beneficial effect, as far as playing, wear, tone or feel is concerned, while some of them have been crafty advertising ploys – the equivalent of a soap manufacturer's "now better than ever" banter.

My advice here is not to take too much notice of manufacturers' claims in the early stages of your string purchasing. As I've said previously, all you've got to worry about is buying electric strings for electric guitars and acoustic strings for acoustic. The rest of it you can safely ignore for now. You'll become choosier as you progress as a musician.

# time for a change?

Another frequently asked question is "How do I know when it's time to change my guitar strings?". Now, this question is asked most often by people who have remembered that their strings were once all bright and shiny, where now they are black or dark brown. Unfortunately, the answer isn't quite as straightforward as you'd like it to be, because people wear out strings at very different and highly individual rates.

It can even depend on body chemistry. One of the principal factors that affects string life is corrosion from sweat – and some of us sweat more (and some more corrosively!) than others. Some players pick the strings much harder than others, literally giving the strings a harder time, and this can dramatically shorten their lives, too.

So it's very difficult to peg a single answer onto the question. The best way of looking at it is to compare a set of strings to a stick of chewing gum. There comes a point, when you're chewing gum, when all the flavour's gone and all you've got left is just a chewable, rubbery glob.

It's the same thing with guitar strings. After a few

weeks (or sometimes hours) of being bashed around onto metal frets and sweated upon, strings lose their brightness. Literally, it's like someone's turned all of the treble down on your hi-fi – the guitar sounds like it's lost a lot of tone.

The main problem here is that this process can happen so slowly that the loss in treble is all but imperceptible, so you decide that all's well and you might as well leave things as they are.

So by far the most reliable way to answer the "when to change?" question is to say that, if you see any discolouring, you've left it too late. If your guitar is beginning to sound like it's lost its brightness, it's definitely time to go down to the guitar shop.

# is your guitar on your side?

It might come as something of a shock to realise that your brand-spanking-new, dream machine of a guitar might need some fine-tuning before it's ready, able and willing to give you its best. Just like buying a suit off the peg in a high-street store, you can expect to find a few nips and tucks necessary before everything is as it should be and your guitar responds favourably to your every embrace.

Guitar manufacture has come along in leaps and bounds over the past ten years or so, to the point where it's comparatively unlikely that you'll end up with a real dog-in-a-box instead of a faithful and loving pedigree of an instrument, so there's usually nothing too serious that you're required to do in order to get everything up and running nicely.

I saw some real nightmares during the 1980s. Students would come to me to learn guitar and reel with horror when I told them that the biggest factor operating against their learning to play well was their brand-new pride and joy. Several of these monstrosities needed some pretty extensive work done on them before they were tamed sufficiently to enable any serious progress – and I wish I had £10 for every time someone asked me why quality control wasn't more stringent during manufacture, etc. Sometimes we even evoked the guarantee, things were so bad.

Still, don't be put off. Like I say, things have got a lot better since then. Even so, it might be worth asking if the shop where you intend to buy a new instrument will include a basic "set-up" in the price. Many will do so with a smile, but be very suspicious if a set-up costs extra – it shouldn't.

# setting up your guitar

Let me just say, before we proceed too far along this particular path, that any work carried out on an instrument should be undertaken by a qualified professional. Oblique shots in the dark will only do more harm and cost more to put right in the long run, so be warned!

We'll just have a look at some of the things that could effect the overall playability of your guitar. Actually getting them sorted out, meanwhile, will need an experienced touch.

# action

You'll hear the world *action* bandied about in guitar circles quite frequently. The term refers to the height of the strings above the neck and is, therefore, quite a determining factor in the general "feel" of an instrument.

A high action can sometimes be a serious handicap, especially for the guitar novice. Strangely enough, a low action can often get in the way, too, as it affects techniques such as bending strings. Bending a string with too low an action can cause the string to grind on the neck and "choke off" the note.

# highs and lows

Obviously, the determining factor here is how you define high and low, and so let's look at how this all-important statistic is measured.

If you turn your guitar so that you're looking at a side view of the neck, you should be able to see that there is a gap between the tops of the frets and the undersides of the strings. If you count up to the twelfth fret (the one with the double dot beside it) and look at the distance between the top of the fret and the string, you should be looking at a gap of around $4/_{64}$ to $6/_{64}$ of an inch on the bass side and $3/_{64}$ to $4/_{64}$ on the treble. This sort of measurement represents normal or standard playing action. Obviously, anything greater would be deemed as being high, while anything less would be seen as low.

In general, you want to aim for a standard action to begin with, and so, if your guitar falls outside these parameters, it might be worth experimenting. Adjustment is usually done at the bridge via some form of specialised tool.

If you own an acoustic guitar, then I'm afraid it's a trip to the guitar shop for you, because adjusting the string height on an acoustic is definitely not a job for the uninitiated.

# nuts

The other factor that can influence string height is the
nut, found up at the other end of your guitar. In an ideal
world, the string slots in your guitar's nut should be cut
so that they fit your chosen string gauge snugly, and
they should also be cut to the right height, but in the
real world string slots are often cut too high and need
slight adjustment. It's no good making any string height
adjustments down at the bridge if the strings are still
too high at the other end as this will have pretty much
no effect on the guitar's playability in this respect.

As a rough guide, hold down the bass E string at the
first fret. If the string now forms a dramatic angle with
the nut at the point where it passes through it, the
chances are that your nut hasn't been cut deeply
enough. If this is the case, DON'T ATTEMPT TO CUT IT
YOURSELF! Seriously, this is a one-way ticket to some
serious sorrow, as any mistakes will result in nothing
more or less than you having to fork out for a new nut.
Instead, take your guitar to a repairman and let him
decide whether any adjustment is necessary.

# truss rods

A truss rod isn't the surgical appliance it sounds like;
it's actually a steel rod that passes through the length

of the neck of your guitar to keep it straight. Guitar strings cause a surprising amount of pull when tensioned up to the point where they're in tune (approximately 16lbs per string), and that pull is trying to distort the playing surface of the guitar by pulling it upwards. The truss rod is there to counterbalance this tension and make sure that the neck stays straight.

Sometimes, even in new instruments, this compromise between push and pull gets out of whack and the guitar neck visibly bows (ie it takes on the contours of a banana) or crowns (ie it becomes slightly convex). In either case, a few adjustments to the truss rod can usually sort matters out in a couple of minutes. But again, ADJUSTING A TRUSS ROD ISN'T SOMETHING YOU SHOULD ATTEMPT YOURSELF! Once again, if you have reason to believe that your guitar neck is being bent out of shape, take it to someone who can, at very least, assure you that you're imagining things and curse me for pointing out that such things can happen.

Other factors that can have an influence over general playability can be almost invisible to the uninitiated and only a trained eye can track them down and know enough to remedy them. One of the first things I do when confronted by a pupil with a gleaming new guitar in his or her hands is check it for flaws that I consider serious enough to warrant attention. Learning to play is a hard enough job to begin with. You don't want your guitar fighting against you every step of the way!

# changing to a different string gauge

Now that we've had a quick look at matters that can turn your guitar from a dream instrument into a nightmare, it's time to return briefly to the subject of strings.

If, for any reason, you want to move up or down in string gauge, remember that the chances are that your guitar was originally set up for the strings it had on it in the shop. Anything you do to it might call for a couple of tweaks just to accommodate its new state. For instance, stepping up a string gauge will put a certain amount more pull on the guitar neck, and so it's possible that the truss rod might need adjusting slightly to correctly counterbalance things once more.

Also, the width of a different string might call for the slots in the guitar's nut to be widened to prevent the strings from sticking and causing all sorts of annoying tuning irregularities.

I know I'm repeating myself, but any adjustments like this should only be carried out by a professional. Tinkering is strictly off limits.

# tremolo units

One of the most dramatic effects that a change in string gauge can have on a guitar takes place down at the tremolo unit. Fender-style tremolos, in particular, are based on a system where string tension is counterbalanced by spring tension (there are springs attached to the underside of the guitar bridge), and an increase in tension can make some alarming things happen. For a start, it can make your guitar bridge stand up on tiptoe because the springs at the back of the bridge are no longer acting as an exact counterweight. A couple of minutes with a screwdriver (in experienced hands!) will put matters back to normal, but this problem can be upsetting if you're not ready for it.

In just about all other respects, a guitar is not a demanding creature to look after. In truth, it needs very little in terms of care and attention. However, it's a good idea to wipe the playing surfaces (strings, neck, etc) with a dry cloth after a practice session and invest in a case to protect it from knocks and bumps, as well as a good strap to keep it securely around your neck, and it's always best to use a little forethought before walking through doorways with your guitar hanging around your neck. You'd be surprised how many accidents have been caused to guitar necks in this way!